Self-Esteem

Strategies for Breaking Free from the Labyrinth of
Overthinking and Paving the Way to Clear Thinking,
Mastery, and Self-Assurance

*(Develop the Skill to Love Oneself and Live in Harmony
with Oneself)*

Julian de Zwart

TABLE OF CONTENT

Talk More Gently And Pause More 1

What Is The Subject Matter Of This Book? 13

Acquiring The Ability To Accept Yourself...................27

Developing The Correct Attitude: Your Success And Happiness Road Map 55

Knowledge Of Poor Self-Esteem 78

Work-Life Balance And Self-Care 94

What Is Self-Compassion? 104

The Relationship Between Self-Esteem And Confidence 146

Talk More Gently And Pause More

Unless you're Tony Robbins or Les Brown, in which case you speak too quickly out of fear that someone else would make fun of you, you speak too quickly. You had a sneaking suspicion that they would enter and remove me. For you, this might be the case. We can slow down our progress downstairs. You view the idea as an extremely helpful slow-down inducement. You're moving too fast because you think someone might interrupt you. Who or what is concerned? Regardless of how fast you're talking, they will cut you off if they're being impolite or find you to be incredibly boring. They weren't really listening if you hurried when they could have skipped into the finish of your statement. This is noticed by the great majority of individuals who are curious about what you're doing. It's okay if they jump in if you stop. It's not a monologue; it's a dialogue. Together, you develop an interest in a concept. So go ahead and assert it. Go easy on yourself. Have you noticed that we have a bad habit of talking nonstop? We can't even stop talking if we don't know what to say; we're just filling the air with ums and uhs and other inane words. Hearing someone use three mums in a row is not only unpleasant, but it also shows that they are missing a fantastic opportunity. You would have more time to consider what they are trying to say right away if they took out all the filler words and substituted them with pauses. Allow your imagination to create a lovely picture.

Right after "tired," when he initially paused, you had time to think. It's a challenge that you don't have someone to talk to about something that is happening to you and to everyone else. You consider it to be quite essential. For the next two breaks, I will continue in the same manner, pausing only to consider and nod after "looking," the 5-second lag becomes very apparent. My thoughts are consumed by my portion of the speech. Trying to get away from how

I'm feeling. He gets to express my emotions instead. Proficient orators employ consistent and purposeful pauses.

Regulate Your Motions

Now, let us consider the language of the body. The National Communication Association's six-point grading scale, which you previously completed, applies to body language: posture, attention, unconscious motions, expressiveness of the face, gestures, and eye contact. That is quite a bit. And currently, we wish to develop each one of them. Therefore, you must act immediately.

Just sit motionless. Put an end to them all. It is important that your hands stay in one place, your legs and feet don't hop, and your eyes don't jump around while you're trying to blink.

Imagine someone who is content and at ease in this location right now. Pay attention to their posture and their facial expression. With our arms comfortably resting on their chair's backrest, we occupy a far larger area than they deserve. They don't seem to be laughing, but they do have a small smile that suggests they're in the middle of a pleasant reminiscence. They have their backs to the chair and are erect but not rigid. You now gradually adapt. They are transitioning to the location you anticipated with gradual, carefree motions from their state of immobility. What is his emotional state? In what way do you think you're seeing? For this final experiment, why do you suppose someone who is at ease and at ease will lean in to give more attention? Will they gaze at you, smile, and bend forward to clasp their hands under their mouths? Will they listen intently as they bend in your direction, laying one elbow on your arm and their chin on one side? As you enter the relaxed pose, try to take one gentle stride into the stance. What was the feeling behind that?

Even though you may already feel really uneasy, you may also feel more composed, in control, and even a little smooth. Subconsciously, you are mimicking real-life individuals or fictional characters that possess similar traits. As unsettling as that may sound, two different meta-studies that looked at the effectiveness of more than 38 training programs show that emulation is among the most evidence-based learning strategies. It functions. Whenever you feel like it, perform the simple exercise again. Try it alone in a restaurant or coffee shop and start holding it up. On your friends, use it. It only takes one easy exercise to create any major body language category.

Establish Eye Contact

When you are having a conversation, how do you look? It's a really widespread issue. The bad news is that everything you've said so far about fundamental counsel is accurate.

You have to maintain eye contact to initiate a conversation. You can look the other person in the eye 90% of the time during the conversation. Make eye contact and smile at the same time. People's initial unease in social situations is a major contributing factor to their concern over maintaining eye contact. They ask where to look, what to say to fill the emptiness, and what to do with their faces. They need to consider it because we feel uncomfortable. They fidget more and more fearfully when they are apprehensive, as seen by their hands, eyes, and faces.

How, then, can you improve eye contact? Observe the fundamental laws outlined above. Gaze your companion in the eyes, feign a half-smile, and only avert your gaze out of want rather than habit. Take action and give it some thought for a week. You will eventually revert to your old behaviors, but you will do so with a slight improvement. Occasionally, you will realize that you're not very good at it, and you'll waste another week staring into people's faces, trying to figure out if you appear abnormal or not.

And that's exactly how this procedure operates. If you're feeling pretty at ease, try these suggestions to improve eye contact: eye contact can make some individuals anxious, but usually only if your face is expressionless. You'll be fine if you just smile or answer anything they say. That's one of the very few errors you can make when it comes to eye contact.

You speak with your eyes instead of staring. Share this if you're content. If you're astonished or furious, use your eyes to communicate your feelings with aggression. It's a small game, but it's more entertaining than glancing at someone's nose bridge and wondering whether they're moisturizing. When at a gathering, glance at more than just the person speaking. Take in your surroundings and occasionally look one or two other partygoers in the eye. Since you are the talk's conductor, be sure you are aware of what occurs to the other actors. How do they feel? They appear inactive, don't they? See, do they have anything else to say? Could you please simplify this?

It's comforting to know that your eye movements are real and not tricks. This is not a personality characteristic. This is not a triumphant moment. It's simply an additional facet of getting to know someone else, having a good rapport with you, and understanding what they're talking about.

What Is The Subject Matter Of This Book?

In a nutshell, this book is a route to happiness, success, and love. It aims to give each of us—a wide range of distinct creatures confronting distinct challenges—the knowledge and abilities to muffle the cacophonous clamors of worry, anxiety, and pessimism. This book is a call to action that promotes self-awareness, the breaking through of the cycle of adversity, and alignment with the constant pulse of energy that permeates the universe. My wish? Will you become aware of your own capacity for rebirth after being motivated by your newly acquired knowledge?

An Image Created Through Experience

These pages are full of true stories, stories of people just like you who once struggled to break free from the anchor-like weight of everyday anxieties and challenges because they were caught in the web of their own negative thoughts. Christine was an artist, but she was engulfed in a maelstrom of fear and self-doubt that kept her from realizing her potential. Throughout her artistic path, this book gave her fresh insight. She reappeared, transformed, a luminous individual full of confidence whose art now exudes joy and love.

John, a middle-aged man stuck in his boring life, discovered the language of the cosmos through this book, just like Christine. His life was completely changed by it, breaking through the glass ceiling of fear and passivity and providing opportunities for achievement, adventure, and the discovery of new passions. My inspiration for writing this novel came from their tales, which are interwoven throughout.

Recognitions

We are incredibly grateful to the numerous scientists, philosophers, spiritual guides, and laypeople who have devoted their lives to comprehending and disseminating the wisdom of the universe so that we can all experience its core. The development of this book was greatly influenced by the writings of great minds, including Rumi, Albert Einstein, and Carl Jung. And coworkers who provided constant encouragement, scathing criticism, and anecdotes throughout the writing of this book.

Our Collective Adventure

There's a reason you picked this book to read, and for that, you have my profound thanks. You've come here in search of something more, a fresh perspective on the world, and I'm here to accompany you on every step of the route.

This book is meant for all kindhearted people who are prepared to take the less-traveled path in pursuit of happiness, unwavering love, and long-term success. To understand this information, all you need is an open mind and the desire to go beyond where you are right now.

Simple or complex, brief or extended, our adventure will be illuminating. We shall uncover layers of self-awareness, dip our toes into the enlightenment river, and clear the cobwebs of anxiety and fear.

I, the work's author, kindly request that you take the time to fully immerse yourself in the experience. There is no hurry; metamorphosis is an ongoing process rather than a final destination. Have faith in the process and realize that obstacles are really opportunities for growth.

I'm grateful. You've made the first move towards more happiness, love, and success by selecting this book. I now extend an invitation to you to read on, to cling to that flicker of interest, and to let it guide you towards the finish line, where the solutions you seek are waiting for you with open arms. You will get closer to the answers you seek with every page you turn, the concept you grasp, and the approach you employ.

Together, let's go off on this adventure.

4. Differentiating between Interests and Positions

Positions and interests are two ideas that usually take center stage in the dance of negotiation but are frequently misinterpreted or confused. Their difference is minute yet crucial, impacting the direction and result of talks. This chapter will go into great detail about these ideas, explaining their importance and providing advice on how to use them wisely in any kind of negotiation.

Definitions: Interests vs. Positions

- Posts: These are the specific positions or requests that a side makes during a negotiation. It's the overt request or declaration, the visible tip of the iceberg.

For example, a job can say, "I want a salary of $100,000."

- Interests: These stand for the fundamental needs, wants, anxieties, or concerns that motivate a stance. Using the earlier example, the motivations for the wage demand could be things like maintaining a particular lifestyle, acknowledging expertise, or ensuring financial security.

The Comparison of Icebergs

Consider an iceberg. The area that is visible above the water symbolizes the position, while the large structure underneath it indicates the interest. The true depth and intricacy of negotiation often lay in the area of interest, much as most of an iceberg's mass is below the surface.

The Value of Differentiating the Two- Getting Past Deadlocks: Talking only about positions can lead to deadlocks in talks very rapidly. Finding and comprehending the underlying interests can lead to innovative solutions that meet the fundamental requirements of both sides.

- Forging Better Bonds with Others: Acknowledging and verifying the interests of the other side promotes mutual understanding, respect, and trust, which opens the door to cooperative rather than combative talks.

- Reaching Win-Win Results: Negotiators are more likely to find win-win solutions that meet the underlying requirements of all parties when they are attuned to interests rather than fixated on positions.

Methods for Discovering Interests

- Pose Inquiring Questions: Investigate the "why" rather than the "what," or the stance. You can uncover underlying interests by asking questions like "What concerns lie behind this request?" or "Why is this important to you?"

- Pay Attention Intentionally: As was covered in the last chapter, understanding the feelings and reasons behind a position can be achieved through active listening.

-Express Your Personal Interests: Establishing a transparent tone through candid communication of your own underlying interests can foster reciprocity.

The Drawbacks of Exaggerating Positions

- Restricted Options: Fixing on stances can narrow the scope of potential solutions, possibly causing one or both sides to miss out on options that could work better.

- Increased Conflict: Tensions can rise when people tenaciously hold onto their positions, transforming cooperative conversations into hostile standoffs.

-Lost Possibilities: Negotiators risk missing opportunities for long-term partnerships, synergies, or mutual profits if they don't explore interests.

Use in Practice: Interest-Based Bargaining

This strategy, also referred to as "principled negotiation," places a strong emphasis on finding common ground, distancing oneself from the issue, and concentrating on interests rather than positions. It fosters the notion that, with comprehension and ingenuity, all sides may gain from talks and that they can be more than zero-sum games.

In the context of negotiation, differentiating between views and interests is like tuning into different frequencies. Although stances provide a foundation, the actual magic and promise of negotiation happen in the space of interests. Through comprehension, appreciation, and skillful navigation of these depths, negotiators can convert talks from transactional exchanges into enlightening, mutually beneficial experiences.

Not only is what is being addressed important in the art of negotiation but also how it is discussed. Negotiators might follow many paths to possible success using distributive and integrative techniques. Negotiators can successfully negotiate the complexity of any agreement by knowing the subtleties of these methods and knowing which ones to use with skill. This will ensure that outcomes are resonant with clarity, justice, and mutual profit.

Acquiring The Ability To Accept Yourself

Have you ever offered someone your services with no expectation of anything in return? The best part is that anyone can do it, and it's a real confidence booster. You are demonstrating to yourself that you are competent at something and that you have a good side to your personality by doing things like lending a helping hand at the neighborhood dog shelter or helping the elderly woman next door with her groceries. It's not about bragging, so don't do it for that reason. It's all about the satisfying feeling you receive from convincing yourself that you are valuable.

Avoid taking action just because you feel compelled to. People frequently utilize those who struggle with self-esteem because they are convenient to use. Saying "No" and keeping your head up is simpler, though, if you have an appointment at the nearby dog shelter. People will start to respect you, and you will start to feel some self-respect once they realize you are not going to sit down and do all of their dirty jobs for them. The goal of this activity is to provide you with a sense of purpose—something that all people need.

Giving, whether it be through volunteering at the neighborhood soup kitchen or helping a neighbor with her overgrown garden, makes you feel like you're making a difference in the world. It is crucial to keep in mind that if there are any conditions, the gesture won't be as effective.

You can start to like who you are by doing a few additional things, which are as follows:

Acknowledging your positive attributes

Increasing the amount of time you spend with people you enjoy

Acknowledging that unfavorable people's opinions are unimportant

You are surrounded by people who minimize you. These might be relatives. I recall having similar feelings towards members of my family, but I soon discovered that our interactions were restricted and that if I just didn't bite back when they made fun of me, it would take away from their enjoyment. You know, individuals who are critical of you typically have their own problems, so showing empathy for them instead of making them feel inferior is the preferable course of action. It makes you feel better about who you are and enables them to stop being so harsh. Just don't let someone take advantage of or mistreat you. Show them that their statements reveal more about them than about you by turning away from them.

Creative hobbies that focus your mind on good topics are other things you may do to make yourself feel better about yourself. For instance, you might want to create something. Even if you don't succeed, the act of creating allows you to decompress and feel better about life. You might have certain hobbies that you really enjoy. Instead of allowing other people to influence your actions, stop telling yourself that you don't deserve to enjoy life and start treating yourself to the things you enjoy. Enjoying a favorite movie moment with friends who share your interests or taking some time for self-care, such as getting a facial or pricey hair conditioner, can also lift your spirits. You are valuable. People who struggle with low self-esteem frequently don't think they are and underindulge in their own needs. Be proud of your entitlements. Have fun and engage in activities that lift your spirits.

Allow me to elaborate on the potency of the law of attraction. You attract folks who like to walk over other people if you are one of those people who allow others to walk over you. If your actions are motivated by bringing happiness into their lives, you will probably draw in like-minded others and form friendships with upbeat people, which will strengthen your sense of inner stability and self-worth. You have the right to enjoy life, and as long as you're doing it for your own enjoyment and sense of self, it's acceptable if your tastes are a little odd or if you want to do things that other people don't. Avoid trying to surprise people or acting in a way that just makes other people respond. Give up trying to win people over and start being yourself and accepting who you are. When you suddenly understand that you are worthy and that you have no need to answer to anyone else, that is when self-love takes place. On the day this occurs, you will really wake up looking forward to your plans for the day rather than waiting for other people to force things onto you.

Go ahead and pick wildflowers and enjoy the beauty of nature if that's how you want to spend the afternoon. Go ahead and ride your bike in the park if you want to. Nobody should ever deny themselves the opportunity to pursue their happiness. There is a balance, or scale, in life. The things we must do in order to live simply are on one side. The enjoyable activities we enjoy doing that give us a sense of purpose and fulfillment in life are on the other side. If the scales are off, all you have to do is put more weight on the side of the scale that brings you joy and happiness and quit doing some of the negative things that make you miserable. You'll discover that you take charge of your happiness and don't allow outside influences to tarnish it. This seeming propensity to be cheerful may even make other people want to be friendly with you. Increase the amount of time you spend with people who value your uniqueness since their opinions will boost your self-esteem. Although you are just as valuable as everybody else, your lack of confidence stems from the fact that you pay more attention to outside voices than to your inner guidance.

You just need to choose what's fantastic for you among the many amazing experiences that are out there. Give it your all if it means dedicating time to the care of homeless dogs. You will see a side of yourself that others may not notice, and self-approval is excellent for the soul, so if it means serving soup to the homeless, go ahead and do it. I didn't need to brag to others about it because, trust me, I've been there and experienced that warmth within. It was just a matter of demonstrating to myself that I still have something valuable to contribute. It brings out the best in me on the inside, and it can do the same for you.

Why is self-confidence necessary?

A person cannot lead a happy life if they lack self-confidence. They are troubled by melancholy, discontent, and negativity all the time. They are incapable of having fulfilling relationships. Numerous things, including parenting, early experiences, friendship groups, religious sermons, and education, could be to blame for this. A child raised in a foster family would undoubtedly view the world in a different way than a child raised by loving parents. It is important to remember that your life is ultimately shaped by your self-perception.

aids in the development of your personality

Self-assurance has a role in defining your personality. You strike me as a kind and amiable individual. A person with confidence can take on the world. As long as they're prepared to face the world with optimism, he or she can have anything they desire. Their ability to overcome adversity contributes to their success.

To succeed in the endeavors you undertake

A self-assured individual never wavers from being modest and grounded. This facilitates clear thinking, realism, and appreciation of the situation. All of this results in success and celebration. Being confident in yourself does not imply being arrogant or complacent. It facilitates living a happy life.

Acquire stress management skills.

Many people experience sadness and depression as a result of low self-esteem. These folks are dissatisfied with life and feel lost. Some even go so far as to take their own lives. Being confident in oneself can aid in self-love. You experience acceptance and love. This sensation prompts optimistic thinking, and you proceed in a contented manner. You can determine your level of self-confidence by asking yourself the following questions:

Some indicators that you're confident are:

Are people able to like me?

Me? Who am I?

Do I deserve to be loved?

Do I have a right to happiness?

Do I require other people's assurances?

Do I stay away from people?

How Do You Become More Confident?

Affirmations can help you develop self-worth.

Unknowingly or knowingly, every thought that crosses your mind is an affirmation. Each and every conversation you have with yourself is an affirmation. Nevertheless, they become your daily affirmations when you begin to systematically, consistently, and with a definite objective in mind affirm your views.

For this reason, it's wise to monitor your thoughts. The subconscious is incapable of distinguishing between good and wrong. It only requires acting on the ideas or words. On the other hand, these same phrases, when stated deliberately, thoughtfully, and often, are referred to as daily affirmations, and they assist you in achieving your goals. It's possible to revamp your life by changing the uncontrollably occurring thoughts in your head to positive affirmations! There are techniques to monitor your thoughts and turn all of the useless information into useful knowledge. While practicing meditation might yield similar outcomes, with a little effort and time, anyone can use this straightforward and powerful method of making affirmations every day to alter the course of their life.

Using affirmations might make you feel as though you are in control of your own future. That boosts your self-assurance. Self-esteem rises when you recognize that you have a purpose in life.

Put an end to self-doubt.

The adage "what goes around, comes around" has probably been heard a lot. What does this signify? It means you have to be ready to get in return for your efforts. Good deeds yield good deeds, and negative deeds yield precisely that! Thus, start by critically analyzing your thoughts first. Do they exhibit strength and decisiveness or weakness and positivity? Recognize every idea you have since it influences your behavior and, in the end, determines the quality of your life. Your life will be more successful and positive the more forceful and positive your thoughts are. Simply dismiss any negative thinking as soon as it arises! You have two options: mentally place a large cross on it or simply blast it high into the sky! In any case, you should attempt to cancel it fully.

Hypnosis for therapeutic purposes

To maximize performance, work on focus, self-assurance, and stress management while in a hypnotic state.

The following is how hypnosis can be applied to improve performance:

Boost self-confidence: Hypnosis is a useful tool for cultivating a positive outlook and increasing self-confidence. It is possible to increase confidence in one's capacity and capacity for success by employing hypnotic suggestions.

Handling performance-related stress and anxiety: Deep relaxation methods that assist in lowering tension and anxiety before a performance can be taught through hypnosis. This can enhance mental serenity and focus throughout the activity.

Visualizing Optimal Performance: You can use visualization to conjure up strong images of success and peak performance when you're in a trance. This mental preparation can enhance real performance in an artistic or competitive setting.

Pain and Injury Management: Performers or athletes can use hypnosis to control their pain or heal from injuries more quickly and efficiently.

Boost concentration: During a performance, hypnosis can assist in reducing distractions by enhancing mental focus and concentration.

Creating Coping Mechanisms: Hypnosis can be utilized to create mechanisms to help get over emotional or mental barriers that could impair performance.

Working with a certified hypnotherapist is essential for getting the most performance-enhancing effects since they can customize the method to your unique needs and track your development over time. Your performance in a variety of areas can be greatly enhanced by consistently using the methods you learned during hypnosis sessions.

Hypnosis is an effective technique for overcoming a variety of personal obstacles as well as improving performance in the arts and sports. To customize the strategy and guarantee success, it is essential to precisely define the objectives you wish to accomplish and collaborate with a qualified hypnotherapist.

As a fundamental element of hypnosis, suggestions are essential in molding the subconscious into new emotional states, cognitive patterns, and desired actions. Although using recommendations requires consistent work and practice, it can result in long-lasting, beneficial improvements in an individual's life.

Crucially, hypnosis needs to be used responsibly and under the guidance of a professional. You can be guided through the procedure, have sessions customized to meet your needs, and have your progress tracked by a certified hypnotist. Under appropriate supervision and methodology, hypnosis can be shown to be a highly beneficial instrument for bringing about constructive transformation, accomplishing individual objectives, and enhancing overall wellness.

Opening up to the possibility of hypnosis under the guidance of a qualified professional and with an open mind can lead to new opportunities for wellbeing and personal development.

Give Yourself Some Time.

While it might not be the first thing that comes to mind when thinking about boosting confidence, it's true that if your fundamental needs aren't being satisfied, it can be difficult to feel good about yourself. Your level of self-assurance serves as a gauge of your social, mental, physical, and spiritual wellbeing. Thus, make sure you're taking proper care of yourself by getting enough exercise, finding time for your interests, connecting with others, and so on.

A vital component of our life, self-care is crucial for boosting self-esteem and confidence. Building a healthy and solid foundation for our lives is possible through self-care, and this is crucial for boosting self-esteem and confidence. Let's discuss how developing our own space, connecting with others, engaging in personal interests, getting enough exercise, and using other self-care techniques can help us feel more confident and good about ourselves.

Getting Adequate Movement: As previously mentioned, research has demonstrated that physical activity and exercise improve mental health, including self-esteem and confidence. Physical activity causes our bodies to create endorphins, which are feel-good and mood-enhancing substances. Exercise also aids in lowering tension and anxiety, two factors that are known to have a significant role in low self-esteem and confidence. Our confidence and self-esteem can be positively impacted by frequent movement, which can also improve our general mental health and wellbeing.

Setting Up Our Personal Space: In the fast-paced world of today, feeling overburdened and stressed out is common. Reducing stress and enhancing our mental health need us to make time for ourselves and make space for self-care. Taking time for ourselves, whether it be by reading a book, going for a stroll, or having a relaxing bath, allows us to revitalize and recharge, which is crucial for boosting our self-esteem and confidence.

Connecting with Others: Our mental health and general wellbeing are greatly influenced by the relationships we have with other people. Our sense of belonging, which we get from connecting with others, can increase our self-esteem and confidence. For a solid foundation of confidence and self-worth, establishing connections with others is crucial, whether through volunteering, socializing with strangers, or just spending time with friends and family.

Scheduling Personal Hobbies Time: Taking up personal interests and hobbies is a great method to enhance our wellbeing and mental health. Painting, writing, playing an instrument, taking up a new activity, or even enrolling in an art class are examples of hobbies that can make us feel happier and more fulfilled with our lives, which is important for boosting our self-esteem and confidence.

In summary, self-care is an important part of our lives and is crucial for boosting self-esteem and confidence. Building a healthy and solid foundation for our lives is possible through self-care, and this is crucial for boosting self-esteem and confidence. Taking care of oneself is essential for laying a solid foundation of confidence and self-esteem, whether that is finding time for personal hobbies, interacting with people, getting enough movement, or making space for ourselves.

Developing The Correct Attitude: Your Success And Happiness Road Map

Developing Resilience

The capacity to adjust and prosper in the face of difficulty is known as resilience. It's an essential ability for developing the proper mindset because it allows you to overcome obstacles and disappointments. The following are techniques for enhancing resilience:

1. Create a Robust Support System: Nurture connections with peers, mentors, family, and friends who can offer emotional support in trying times.

Resilience is built on a solid network of supportive individuals.

2. Engage in Self-Care: Make self-care activities that enhance mental and physical health a top priority and practice relaxing methods like deep breathing or meditation.

3. Develop Emotional Intelligence: This entails identifying and comprehending both your own and other people's feelings. It gives you the ability to act with empathy and self-awareness in difficult situations.

4. Set Achievable and Realistic Goals: Make sure your objectives are in line with your values and skills. Setting

unrealistic expectations could weaken resilience and cause disappointment.

5. Adapt to Change: Accept change as an inevitable aspect of existence. Be adaptable and receptive to new things. People who are resilient are flexible and able to flourish in changing circumstances.

6. Develop Problem-Solving Skills: By dissecting difficulties into smaller, more doable steps, you can improve your problem-solving skills. Adopt an approach focused on finding solutions to challenges.

7. Learn from Adversity: See hardship as a teaching opportunity. Think back on your previous struggles and the lessons

you took away. Make the most of these lessons to strengthen your resilience and deal with hardship in the future.

8. Keep a Positive Attitude: Resilience and positivity go hand in hand. Even in the midst of hardship, maintain hope and optimism. Instead of focusing on issues, consider possibilities and solutions.

9. Engage in Mindfulness Practice: During trying circumstances, mindfulness may keep you centered and in the moment. It makes it possible for you to better control your emotions and stress.

Creating Opportunity Out of Adversity

When faced with the appropriate mindset, adversity can spur development and transformation. Adversity should not be seen as a barrier but rather as a chance to grow and succeed. Here's how you can use hardship to your advantage:

1. Modify Your Viewpoint: Reframe how you see hardship. Consider it a challenge or a step towards your objectives rather than a setback.

2. Look for the Silver Lining: There is usually a bright side to every hardship. Seek out the good things or things you may learn from difficult circumstances.

3. Adapt and Innovate: Adapting to adversity frequently calls for innovation

and adaptation. Adversity can serve as a spark for innovative problem-solving and fresh approaches to obstacles.

4. Foster Resilience: Experienced hardship fosters resilience. Seize the chance to build up your resilience muscles and improve your ability to handle obstacles in the future.

5. Set New Objectives: You might need to redefine your objectives in the face of adversity. When it comes to reassessing your goals and changing directions, be willing to adapt.

6. Seek Support: In difficult times, rely on your network of allies. Talk to people you can trust for advice and support when you share your struggles.

7. Accept Change: Adversity frequently brings about change. Accept change as a chance for both professional and personal development. Keep an open mind to potential new experiences and chances.

8. Learn and Grow: Misery teaches us important lessons. Spend some time thinking back on the lessons you've learned and the ways that difficult events have helped you to grow.

9. Remain Persistent: Overcoming hardship requires persistence. Even in the face of setbacks, be dedicated to your objectives and keep moving forward.

10. Appreciate Little Wins: Along the journey, note and commemorate your

little successes. No matter how tiny a step you take, it gets you one step closer to conquering hardship.

Adversity can be turned into an opportunity with the right mindset and a readiness to change and grow from setbacks. You may overcome challenges and turn them into stepping stones toward success and happiness by facing adversity with tenacity and positivity.

In summary, conquering difficulties is a crucial step on the path to developing the proper mindset. The ability to bounce back from setbacks, take constructive criticism and rejection well, develop resilience, and turn adversity into opportunity is crucial for developing a positive outlook and reaching success and happiness. Remember that your attitude is your most valuable resource when you confront problems along the way. It may help you not only overcome obstacles but also flourish in the face of them.

4. ENDING SELF-SABOTAGING

"Avoid undermining yourself. Many others are willing to perform such service at no charge.— Jenny Lawson

How often have you lamented that you are unlucky in love after making completely poor romantic choices?

Think about the times you have followed a rigorous, calorie-restricted diet plan all week just to overindulge in that delectable pepperoni pizza on the weekend. Consider how often you have considered asking your employer for a boost in pay but decided against it since you knew you probably wouldn't receive it.

I believe you understand my point of view. Even though you may WANT to act differently, you choose not to because you believe you are unworthy, incompetent, incapable, or for a variety of other reasons. You actively or inadvertently look for ways to stop yourself from achieving your objectives and desires rather than going after them, and before you know it, you've missed out on chances and fulfilling experiences. When that occurs, you are the one who ridicules yourself the most for not being able to achieve success or fulfillment, and the whole thing culminates in a well-known "I told you so" story.

Yes, that does sound strange. But the root of the whole thing is a pessimistic mindset that encourages failure and sets you up for failure. Self-criticism and self-sabotage can ruin you emotionally, psychologically, or physically and damage your prospects of happiness. How? by undermining you and creating obstacles for you to overcome while you work towards your objectives. This chapter is about identifying and putting an end to self-sabotage before it causes you to self-combust. Self-sabotage is dangerous because it is so subtle that you hardly even recognize you are doing it.

Worry is a major factor in many self-destructive behaviors, specifically, the kind of worry that consumes our thoughts, even in the absence of a genuine threat. "I'm not going to make it," and other such negative thoughts might immobilize us, causing us to choose to stray from our objectives rather than move forward. To recognize this process—which is really subtle—you must be aware of your inner self. Your brain frequently fabricates apparent hazards because it is incapable of distinguishing between real and imagined dangers.

As I previously stated, the degree of self-awareness you possess determines whether self-sabotage is conscious or unconscious. Shopping sprees are one instance of purposeful self-sabotage, as you are aware that you will not have enough money for necessities if you indulge in them. Anything that, even though you can't perceive it, compromises your ideals or aspirations could be considered an unconscious example.

You might put off studying for an impending exam until the last minute if you're afraid of failing, which would unintentionally prevent you from succeeding. Self-sabotage can leave you depressed, anxious, and lacking in motivation if you follow it for an extended period of time.

Why do I undermine myself?

The good news is that we are aware of the causes of self-sabotage and have developed strategies for overcoming it in order to adopt a more constructive and optimistic outlook.

It's primarily a biological reaction to potentially dangerous situations, and avoiding them appears like a better course of action. That reveals a lot about your degree of self-worth, and if your mental health isn't excellent, you'll do all in your power to avoid confrontations. It makes logical, and we all engage in it.

Modeling is the term used to describe the process by which we mimic the patterns and models of behavior from our early years. This can also refer to the lack of a suitable model, which prevents us from responding in a way that serves our own interests. You may have been hesitant to push yourself, take risks, or go out without feeling anxious if your overly cautious parent was always concerned that you would become sick.

A parent's rejection might set off a powerful cocktail of relational instability that can cause trust issues. In an attempt to prevent more rejection, this may cause you to undermine your prospects of developing intimate relationships.

If you have gone through trauma in your life, you will probably view the world as dangerous, which you cope with by engaging in self-defeating behaviors like staying home instead of moving to get a better job or even putting your health and welfare last.

Self-sabotage is not limited to women; in fact, we tend to be extremely predictable in the situations we choose to use it. Given how preoccupied we are with our weight and looks, it should come as no surprise that the majority of our life's challenges center on achieving a specific appearance or changing into a specific body type. Like our vocations or jobs, relationships also tend to bring out the worst in our fear-factor behavior. It will be simpler for you to make the necessary changes once you realize that your self-destructive behavior is a direct result of your lack of self-love.

Some possible behaviors that you might exhibit while you work to destroy your own life are mentioned below. I also want you to consider the following consequences that you have gone through:

Pointing up flaws in others

If you enjoy criticizing other people, that allows you to grow and avoid dealing with your own problems. You destroy any opportunity to learn from the experience when your spouse behaves in a way that you find unacceptable, and instead of taking responsibility for your own actions, you choose to end the relationship. Sometimes, there's no one to blame, and life simply gets in the way, but continuously seeking out reasons to break up won't help you create a valuable, long-lasting relationship.

The Perfectionism Issue

Perfectionism is your worst enemy when it comes to will strength. It will condemn, berate, and demoralize you. And all of this is a result of your unrealistic expectations of yourself. Nothing is perfect when you're looking for perfection. As a result, you will fall into a trap and never stop believing that your work is insufficient.

Envisioning yourself as a kind personal trainer who encourages your pupils to make an effort only by praising them for it is a helpful strategy for conquering perfectionism. Another strategy is to purposefully set a very low bar and then congratulate yourself on reaching it. Thus, start small and gradually expand your ambitions. For example, run for five minutes every morning or study five new Spanish words every day for a week.

Perfectionism is a common hindrance to writers; no matter how hard they try, their work never seems to measure up. The "free thinking" or "free writing" approach offers a workaround for this. The author sets aside a certain amount of time, let's say thirty minutes, and just "dumps" everything onto the paper. A free exchange of thoughts merely to get the words out. It will obviously not be flawless, but at least it is available and can be altered as needed. Half the battle is won as long as they have taken action.

Expect Obstacles

Before you go out to achieve your goal, think about everything that could go wrong or divert your attention. Always expect that problems or obstacles may arise, and prepare a strategy for handling them should they arise. It will boost your confidence to know you have a plan in place to handle issues. For instance, plan your food shopping well in advance if your objective is to cook more. Make multiple meals ahead of time to save time if you believe you won't have time to work on your project in the evenings. Make backup plans for child care, or block out a day in your calendar to dedicate yourself fully to achieving your objective.

Asking a member of your support system to check in with you—as opposed to just dropping by—to find out how you're doing and provide you with the necessary encouragement and assistance is another smart move.

Steer clear of temptation.

Not even the strongest among us are immune to temptation. Alternatively, "I can resist anything except temptation," as Oscar Wilde stated. We all have weaknesses, and they're not always negative things. However, if your shortcomings get in the way of your objectives or, worse, make you feel self-conscious, why not make arrangements to avoid encountering them in the first place?

Consider the circumstances you place yourself in. Avoid the dessert and microwaved meal sections at all costs if you're attempting to lose weight. You should also alter your route home to avoid particular locations. This also applies to the people in your inner and outer circles of friendships: stay away from those who you know will drain your energy, be untrustworthy, or betray you.

Knowledge Of Poor Self-Esteem

The most inconvenient times and places are when the demon of low self-esteem makes an appearance in your life. It could show up as hopelessness, anxiety, fear, or completely unimportant ideas. The demon is limitless and has an independent thought process. It will not stop until you recognize its approach, recognize when it is at your door, and force it out of your life. Sometimes, unhealthy self-esteem is subtle and hard to spot.

Unhealthy self-esteem is something that many people understand, but it doesn't always show up in the ways that are typical. Some people think that introverts who don't get out much are the ones that struggle with self-esteem. They believe that people who struggle to uphold their relationships, careers, and houses are frequently involved in harmful, self-destructive behaviors. This is unquestionably untrue. It's true that many people with low self-esteem end up being withdrawn or in bad relationships. However, those who struggle with poor self-esteem are not limited to those who are obviously oppressed.

A low sense of self-worth can seep into many facets of your life. You probably don't realize how many of your problems could be stemming from low self-esteem. If you are cynical, you may occasionally catch yourself acting in a bad way.

Here are a few more examples of how people from all walks of life are impacted by low self-esteem. People who have low self-esteem are more likely to • Put pressure on other people and exhibit dictatorial behavior.

Be demoralized by small mistakes.

• Are resource-poor; • Encourage violence within the family or community; • Draw all attention to their inadequacies, shortcomings, and failures; • Embarrass themselves, whether in jest or in earnest.

Your emotional health might be adversely affected by having a low sense of self-worth. It is imperative that you take care of your worth and obtain the support you need. It takes time to develop self-esteem, but there are steps you can take—which we will go into great detail about—to keep your mental health intact as you work on raising your self-esteem.

Identifying Poor Self-Esteem

You can find people who have low self-esteem everywhere. They work as stockbrokers, attorneys, mechanics, instructors, athletes, and workers in the hotel industry. On the other hand, low self-esteem can take many different forms, and those who suffer from it may label themselves as rebels, victims, or imposters.

Rebels act out to show how low their self-esteem is. They ignore others in an attempt to establish themselves. They are determined to prove that they are above the rules and regulations that everyone else abides by or that they are impervious to them. Buried inside them are feelings of failure that enrage them.

Victims don't appreciate taking accountability for their behaviors or feelings. They see nothing wrong with holding a pity party and are more at ease placing the blame for everything on other factors. Because they regularly give in to pressure from others, victims are generally seen as weak in relationships.

A lot of time and effort is put in by imposters to demonstrate their confidence. Still, they are driven by a deep-seated fear of failing and an enduring desire to succeed. Competitors who compare their achievements to others are often imposters.

A person with low self-esteem may, in general, act immaturely and have low emotional intelligence.

· Take part in actions that harm oneself.

• Easily upset and prone to losing composure.

- Give up their individuality in an effort to "blend in."

- Steer clear of unpleasant situations and circumstances.

- Take delight in the fall from grace or humiliation of others.

- Consistently criticize oneself and other people.

- Be conceited and arrogant.

- React excessively to criticism of any kind.

- Let yourself be sabotaged.

This is merely a small portion of the entire list. Ignoring self-esteem problems often leads to deeper and darker inclinations in people. Unhealthy self-esteem often leads to inappropriate wrath directed at other people. It might be hard to control your anger and even harder to choose where to focus it when you're overflowing with hate and bitterness. Sometimes, violent outbursts occur in people with low self-esteem for no apparent reason. They might go on a tirade at the slightest criticism.

They refuse to accept accountability for the consequences of their own decisions and instead begin blaming others for their situation. They don't care about anyone else since they don't value their own lives. If they don't have something to live for, they can't fathom that others do.

You're Capable of More.

What I enjoy talking about is how I stay committed to leading a conscious life because I know that it's often necessary to stick to routines, rituals, and a range of helpful hints and resources to help us live the kind of lives we say we want to.

I am the first to admit that, despite the fact that my life is not perfect, I am happy every single day—possibly even more so now that I have arrived at this stage. Does this mean that I'm feeling joy and happiness all day long? Of course not! However, I've come to understand that I have the ability to alter my emotions and deal with life's challenges more skillfully.

Most of the materials and stories I provide here are based on my view of life as it is right now. Even while I do occasionally run into problems, I rarely experience extreme emotional suffering. Yes, anxiety. Fury? Of course. Sadness? Without a doubt. I also frequently experience feelings of being overwhelmed, annoyed, fearful, jealous, dissatisfied, and disengaged.

However, I also experience happiness, fun, worthiness, zeal, and other good emotions rather often.

When I tell you that I love my daily life, I'm not just putting that out there as part of my branding. This is a sneak peek at my creative work. This is a conscious attempt on my side to share the knowledge I've gained, not a brag about my accomplishments.

I try not to spend too much time looking back. If we had been friends before 2004, you would have met a woman who wasn't simply depressed. But I was in excruciating, all-consuming pain. I worked out, numbed myself with food and booze, and took antidepressants. My friends weren't truly aware of how bad things had gone as I was raised to believe that it was necessary to live a "happy and picture-perfect life."

My husband was not my comrade but my enemy. I was almost always ashamed of myself because I was dishonest with my own morals.

Although I hold honesty in the highest regard, I have a habit of lying. Because whenever I or any of our girls displayed any weakness, especially in terms of behavioral problems at school, he would be extremely severe in our punishment. His complete lack of affection for anyone who had committed an "infraction," as evidenced by the days or weeks he would go without speaking to them, was what wounded us all the most.

When I finally had enough of barely scraping by and got the courage to file for divorce from him, I was terrified. I thought that now that I had put on the perfect front, "everyone" would see me as a failure.

I was worried about how I was going to pay my bills, raise my two girls, and find myself again. Who was I, after all, if I wasn't a "wife"? Although I was unsure of where to begin, I knew I had to start from the inside out. I had the barest idea that happiness would only come from believing in myself.

I had to work at changing the things about my life and myself that I didn't like. I went to therapy, traveled, read, worked with a coach, went to church, and found the resources that worked for me.

And let me tell you, dear, I made a whole lot of mistakes. There were three steps back and two steps forward in the first few months. I didn't want to consider the possibility until I finally gained traction, and the good days began to exceed the bad ones.

Changes in life came gradually. Every time I made a step forward, I had to choose to stay dedicated to the process of creating the life I wanted to live.

Even while I have hazy memories of those days when my life was very different from what it is today, to be really honest, I don't really remember those days in detail. Because the human mind is so powerful, when we utilize it to create the life we want and stick with it, we forget a lot of the pain we have had in the past.

What we remember are the lessons. Even if we can still glimpse glimpses of the past, there are moments when it feels like we are looking into the lives of others. It is our duty to defend ourselves from the things that can cause us to turn back to our old habits.

Despite how miserable life may be. It's not necessary to accept a life that doesn't align with your desires, regardless of how depressing it may seem or how flawless Instagram may suggest your existence is. The life you want can be created by you.

We frequently cling to our suffering even when things go better because we worry that things won't be the same. Plus, I promise you that the thirty-four-year-old me will always be grateful for the forty-seven-year-old me since the rewards of this life outweigh the effort.

Work-Life Balance And Self-Care

Overview: Juggling Work and Personal Care In the middle of "Think Rich, Grow Rich: Building a Mindset for Wealth Creation," the chapter "Balancing Work and Self-Care" opens, bridging the gap between aspiration and wellbeing. This chapter takes us on a journey that acknowledges the mutually beneficial relationship that exists between achieving financial success and taking care of our physical, mental, and emotional wellbeing. By following the three guiding principles of achieving work-life balance, mindfulness, stress reduction, and prioritizing mental and physical health, we may successfully navigate an environment that fosters creativity, productivity, and prosperity supported by a foundation of holistic well-being.

1. Making physical and mental health a priority The journey begins with the realization that our bodily and emotional wellbeing are our most precious possessions. In the first segment, we discuss how important it is to put self-care first when pursuing wealth building. By realizing that the foundation of long-term success is a sound body and mind, we create the conditions for an abundant life in every way. We learn from anecdotes that highlight the transforming potential of

holistic health that financial success is not an afterthought but rather a prerequisite for maintaining one's wellbeing.

2. Stress Reduction and Mindfulness

As we go further, we uncover the practice of stress management and mindfulness, two vital life skills. In the second part, we explore the technique of developing present-moment awareness, which enables us to face difficulties head-on and remain composed. Learning stress-reduction strategies gives us the fortitude to face challenges head-on without compromising our health.

We discover through stories that highlight the benefits of mindfulness that maintaining our ability to manage stress and keep our composure is crucial for preserving both our personal and professional wellbeing (CHAPTER 8).

3. Attaining Calm in Work and Life

The goal of "Balancing Work and Self-Care" is to achieve work-life harmony—a balance between productivity and rejuvenation, as well as ambition and relaxation. In the third section, we look at methods for balancing career aspirations with personal fulfillment. We dive into the practice of time management, boundary-setting, and soul-nourishing activity prioritization. By presenting actual case studies of people who have attained work-life balance, we expose the reality that prosperity isn't limited to the boardroom but rather encompasses a balanced lifestyle that enhances every aspect of our lives.

In the context of "Balancing Work and Self-Care," we learn that true riches include both material success and overall health. By putting our health first, cultivating mindfulness, and striking a balance between work and life, we can walk a path that improves our quality of life and our monetary gains. Let's acknowledge as we go into this chapter that living an abundant life means honoring the fine balance between ambition and self-care, a dance that, when perfected, propels us to a place of genuine prosperity and deep contentment.

Ask dependable friends and family for their opinions.

Positive and negative feedback are equally necessary for professional and personal development. Seek the opinions of your loved ones and friends; they may have numerous insightful opinions that you are unaware of. They may offer you helpful feedback, support, and insight into your areas of weakness, all of which can greatly aid in your development and increase your self-assurance.

Hold a "positive feedback" document containing remarks and affirmations.

You might forget about the encouraging comments you've had as time goes on. Thus, record all of the compliments you receive in a journal. Read through and keep in mind the encouraging comments in this journal. This can help you turn your attention away from negativity, increase your self-confidence, and make you feel good about yourself.

Establish a daily schedule that encourages well-being.

These can involve engaging in mental and physical activity, getting enough sleep, well-being, taking little pauses, and practicing deep breathing, among other things. Self-confidence is increased by mental and physical wellbeing.

Adopt constructive self-talk when confronting obstacles.

When faced with obstacles, have confidence in your ability to overcome them and in yourself. You won't experience self-doubt or negative thoughts as a result. Recall your earlier triumphs over obstacles and have faith in your ability to conquer this one as well.

Maintaining successful relationships requires a number of important factors, one of which is active listening. Actively listening to others demonstrates your regard for them and your willingness to communicate, both of which contribute to the development of enduring relationships. Having supportive relationships with those around you makes you feel more confident and upbeat.

Be proud of how you look; it conveys respect for yourself.

Getting a good haircut and wardrobe are crucial for increasing self-confidence. Your whole self-image increases when you are happy with how you look. Maintaining a decent look is a sign of self-respect and self-care.

Be in the company of positive individuals who encourage you.

Spend time with positive-minded individuals who can encourage and support you. They can inspire you and aid in improving your general wellbeing and sense of self-worth.

Have reasonable expectations for yourself.

Unrealistic wellbeing causes disappointment and frustration and is a major source of stress. As a result, make attainable and realistic goals. When establishing goals, use the SMART (Specific, Measurable, Achievable, Relevant, Time-bound) approach.

What Is Self-Compassion?

A self-compassionate moment can make all the difference in your day.

A series of these incidents might completely alter your life.

My sense of self was completely upended by the divorce I went through after seventeen years of marriage. In addition to adjusting to life as a single mother of four children, I discovered that being a wife, mother, and teacher constituted the core of my identity. It was time for me to examine my identity closely and prioritize my needs for the first time since being married.

I devoured self-help books, made friends who were nice and encouraging, and discovered how crucial it was to treat yourself with kindness. There were other hiccups along the way, and it was not an immediate triumph. It became easier to treat myself with the same kindness as I did my family and students over time.

I made the decision to return to school and earn my master's degree while continuing to work as a full-time teacher in order to help make ends meet and advance on the pay scale. As if that wasn't difficult enough, I faced another issue at the same time!

My physician called me as I was driving to school to let me know that all of the several tests I had performed had shown that I had multiple sclerosis. I was terrified of this news, and it was upsetting to hear it all by myself while traveling to school. I can still feel my heart beginning to race and my blood starting to get chilly. I wondered what was ahead for me since this illness had claimed the lives of two of my aunts.

I was inconsolable. Even though I was relieved to finally understand what was wrong with me, the diagnosis rocked my world and put my life in danger.

During this time, I needed my self-compassion practice more than before.

Many of the symptoms of MS are only noticeable to me since it is an invisible disease. Others who were unaware that I had MS would criticize and become impatient with me. Even worse, as I grew used to living with MS, there was a chance that I might occasionally become harsh, critical, and impatient with myself.

Fortunately, I had the support system and the habits to help me remember to treat myself with kindness. I began educating myself rather than wallowing in the negative news. I kept myself surrounded by upbeat people and acknowledged every small victory. I gradually came to terms with my new normal and learned to accept my mistakes, frustrations, and shortcomings with grace.

I'm still facing obstacles in my life, but self-compassion has given me the strength to keep moving forward. I began to view my failures as evidence that I am improving, learning, and growing rather than as a weakness. Instead of talking to myself dejectedly, I speak to myself lovingly and encouragingly.

Everybody has times of self-doubt, failure, and hardship in life. We frequently punish ourselves for falling short of our aspirations or ambitions. In these situations, self-compassion can be a very useful tool for helping us change the way we think, deal with challenges, and go forward with greater assurance.

What, though, is self-compassion? We shall examine the three components of self-compassion and their advantages in this chapter. Now, let's get started!

Self-compassion: What Is It?

Being kind and understanding to oneself, especially when facing challenges or failing, is a sign of self-compassion. It's not about putting ourselves down or trying to be flawless.

It is not self-compassion to minimize or deny our errors. It's important to comprehend and embrace them. It's important to acknowledge that errors are inevitable in life and that it's normal to feel upset and let down by them. Being self-compassionate also means realizing that our mistakes do not determine who we are. and that we can grow from them and continue on.

It's about learning to accept and not be critical of our own faults. It's about realizing that we are not alone in our problems and that mistakes are a natural part of being human.

Self-Compassion Does Not Equal Self-Esteem.

Although it is not the same as self-esteem, self-compassion has a significant impact on it. Self-compassion is acknowledging that perfection is unachievable. Self-esteem is feeling good about oneself and one's accomplishments.

Not self-pity is self-compassion.

Additionally, self-compassion differs from self-pity. Self-compassion is acknowledging our difficulties and treating ourselves with kindness, whereas self-pity is feeling sorry for oneself. It is about motivating ourselves to take stock of the circumstances and press on.

Self-indulgence is not the same as self-compassion.

It is a widely held view that motivation requires self-criticism and that excessive self-compassion will result in a lack of will to effect change. Taking care of yourself with kindness is not selfish. Actually, it aids in regulating self-criticism to a healthy degree!

When we lack self-compassion, our inner critic will criticize and chastise us until we become too scared to take another step. Self-compassion transforms our internal scolding into productive feedback.

Building Your Self-Esteem

Few people are aware of the profound impact that low self-esteem may have on a person's life. A mind-boggling nature can be greatly diminished by low self-esteem; it can hinder the development of positive and healthy relationships, prohibit you from obtaining a secure and fulfilling career, and increase your risk of developing behavioral and psychological irregularities. I know that I have experienced some of these outcomes; in fact, it was because of them that I decided to look for a way to raise my self-esteem.

In my opinion, there shouldn't be anyone in this world who has low self-esteem. Unfortunately, though, a lot of the factors that shaped this powerful subject matter are sometimes beyond our control. Thankfully, we are in charge of how we use our sense of self-worth. You have two options: you can spend the rest of your life moping over your poor self-esteem, or you may try to raise it. In any event, you should keep in mind that raising your self-esteem would need a significant amount of effort, dedication, and energy.

How to develop self-esteem step-by-step is an issue that many people wonder about. Unfortunately, there is one subject that is rarely taught in schools that has the potential to have the biggest impact on our lives. For this reason, many of us struggle with this concept long after we reach adulthood. We yearn to behave in a guaranteed and certain way, but we're never provided with the tools to make that happen.

That is not how things have to be. You can become the person you've always wanted to be. Additionally, you can start right now. Focusing on your beliefs is the secret to developing long-lasting trust in yourself. (Plus, thankfully, it's not as difficult as you may think.)

Every aspect of our lives is influenced by our beliefs. They are the inspiration behind our thoughts, our actions, and our level of self-worth. "If you think you can, you can," as Benjamin Franklin once stated. You also can't if you believe you can't."

The way you view yourself and your abilities will determine your extraordinary nature. For instance, if you concede that you're not worthy of advancement, you'll miss opportunities and undermine your efforts. In your personal life, the analogy holds true. You will ultimately attract the opposite person—someone who treats you the way you feel about yourself on the inside—if you don't think you deserve their love and deep regard.

These kinds of activities lead to the belief that you have "verification" of your inadequacy and a rationale for your poor self-esteem. It's a never-ending cycle that can continue indefinitely. The key to breaking the pattern is understanding how to increase one's self-worth and deal with these beliefs at their core. The limiting beliefs that are holding you back must be destroyed in order to create a compelling new set of beliefs.

Usually, the difficulty is in reaching these covered convictions. They frequently have intuition. The secret is to let your mind process things naturally and avoid overanalyzing the process. In order to accomplish this, you essentially need to have your considerations set apart from everyone else's, which isn't often the case in our fast-paced society. But true learning can occur in these quiet moments by themselves.

Have you ever noticed, for instance, that when you're taking a shower, you usually have the best ideas? Or, conversely, after taking a walk through the woods, did you feel completely energized and clear about what you needed to do? This is due to the fact that these are the few places where you may truly be by yourself with your thoughts.

By incorporating more of these wise minutes into your life, you can start to unveil your hidden beliefs. Nor does it have to be a laborious process. Even a few minutes of introspection each day can lead to remarkable shifts in your beliefs and thoughts.

This can be accomplished via reflection, journaling, or engaging in activities specifically designed to reveal these beliefs and provide guidance on how to develop your self-worth. Consider one of these topics, for instance, when you're by yourself thinking about it: Love, career, power, money, relationships, courage, and self-worth. Think about your actual feelings towards the word and what it means to you.

One woman used the word "self-esteem" for this exercise since she consistently struggled with poor self-esteem. After a few moments of quiet contemplation, she was shocked by the thoughts that suddenly occurred to her: conceited, haughty, snobbish, flaunt. She realized that even though she had been working to strengthen her certainty for a while, the negative beliefs she held about certainty had been sabotaging her own efforts behind her back.

Once your true beliefs are exposed, all you have to do is create and reinforce a great deal of compelling beliefs to replace the limiting ones from a long time ago. This ought to be achievable through attestations and maintaining awareness of your thoughts to ensure that outdated beliefs don't creep back into your consciousness.

How to Use Frustration as a Chance to Develop a Growth Mindset and Boost Self-Esteem

Many kids go through a phase where they act as though they detest or find it difficult to engage with a certain subject or activity in school. This is a rather prevalent issue, and many parents are concerned. It might be challenging to decide when and how to step in and make improvements.

We were in this predicament when my daughter Noah turned seven. Certain academic disciplines, like ballet, gymnastics, swimming, tennis, etc., embraced the "growth mindset," but it took some time to recognize that reading and writing had instead given rise to a "fixed mindset." She has had difficulty reading for the past year and has started to progressively fall behind. Although we were aware that she was going through a difficult period, we weren't overly concerned because we understood that every child develops at a different rate. And we had faith that the school system would help and motivate her when she needed it. We also acknowledge that reading is postponed till later generations in certain nations. Perhaps she was simply "not ready."

Furthermore, the situation will be blown out of proportion, and Norr will likely detest reading even more if we jump in and try to solve it right now. Our only wish was for her to detest reading until she reached adulthood. We found ourselves in a challenging predicament since we were unsure of what to do. The issue stems from her dislike of reading. She wasn't just having trouble with the fundamentals; she was also really anxious both when she completed the task and when discussing it, particularly when we were reading together (Nadim).

We both didn't know what was so worrying her and even though we tried our best to cheer her on over the next six months, the issue worsened and ultimately kept us from getting into the school of our choice. We called this the "morning call." Since it appears that Norr is not the only person experiencing this phase, the issue is not resolved. It was actually becoming worse, so this was the right time to take action.

The moment we got down and spoke about how we had handled the matter up to that point, it was evident to us that Norr had no "growth mindset" when it came to reading. Even though we bought time for Carol to read aloud and encouraged her to practice, she was erratic enough to make regular progress. This is very important since she needs to boost her self-esteem and proficiency.

In addition, we talked about what was bothering Noah so much when she read aloud to me. Ultimately, we decided that Noah had been afraid to read to me. Noah needed to know that she could feel better about herself and that mistakes were okay in order for her to read with me more readily. In order to better comprehend her challenges, I had to try to be more patient and less hard on myself.

In this instance, we decided that it would be best to sit down with Noah and let her assist in creating a summer reading program. Engaging her in this manner was a great way to get her to share some of the problems she's been going through. Besides, she knew that if she had any control over her schedule, she would be far more inclined to follow it.

By listening to her and showing more empathy for her attempts, we were able to immediately ascertain that Noah was upset that she was falling behind her children in age. We also learned that her teacher, like INadim at home, would sometimes become irate at Noah's slow reading speed, suggesting that she was afraid of making mistakes and misreading.

Thus, we carried out our plan during the summer vacation. Not all circumstances are clear-cut. There were many power clashes during the process. However,

Carol consciously chose to work very hard to support Noah's career and find a family solution, and I consciously tried to be more patient, understanding, and flexible.

Noah picked up on the fact that our encouragement and support were focused on her progress, and the more reading she did, the better she would become. Adopting this growth mentality took a lot of effort and time, and things didn't get any better.

After months of practice, we gathered on Sundays before school to have family meetings. At the beginning of each meeting, we expressed our appreciation and thankfulness to each other. Noah surprised us all by starting a whole new project. She asked, "Can I thank myself?" "Do you mean you want to share something you're proud of?" we asked. Yes, in fact! Now that Charlie and the Chocolate Factory is over, I've been reading it more and loving it more," she declared with enthusiasm. Carol and I were chuckling uncontrollably! We now carry out her recommendation, which we thought was a great idea, to have her speak about her accomplishments at the family conference. Every week, we find out what each family member is proud of.

Adding even more significance to the problem was the revelation that Noll could not "read normally" due to a real eye disease that she discovered after the experience. Since we thought that her reading issues might be the cause, we've previously had an ophthalmologist check her eyes. Research and consulting with board-certified ophthalmologists were the only means to find out if she passed the exams. When Noah started working out regularly, wearing glasses, and reading books to help with his vision problems, his recuperation went more quickly.

After three months of eye exercises, Noah's reading speed increased significantly. Before, she was slow and needed a lot of skills to absorb the material in the book. She is now reading at a "normal" pace for her age, proving that her hard work and devotion paid off!

What we can learn from these practical experiences

Parents must focus on developing a growth mentality in their children, yet this cannot be achieved by just setting high expectations for them. Praise children for their efforts, growth, and perseverance while showing them that their problems and mistakes are completely "normal" and that they are truly appreciated. This will deter children from taking on new responsibilities and making mistakes.

A low sense of self-worth and confidence will likely present you with many challenges. Acknowledging the potential reality can empower you to cultivate the courage and resilience required to surmount poor self-worth and progress toward a more positive existence. Did you come to that? How does a lack of confidence and poor self-worth work similarly to how a parasite infects a host? Parasites feed on their host once they start to sicken them or, in the worst instance, kill them. Think of parasites like ticks that attach themselves to the body of a defenseless animal and feed on its blood. This is especially a problem for dogs and cows. The animal will never be free and content until the parasites are eliminated from its body. It requires assistance to remove them in order to accomplish this; often, the animal's carers are better able to locate the tick's hiding place than the animal itself.

With human help, the animal can eventually reclaim its freedom and resume a happy, healthy life. The same concept applies to us. Low self-esteem and lack of confidence can suffocate us like a tick on our skin. It drains your joy, irritates you incessantly, and wears you out. Many more aspects of who we are remain hidden from our own perception. Being open to absorbing the frank criticism of others can help you discover where you might have been going wrong, what's causing you distress, and the root of all your worries. It's important to remember that you don't have to improve yourself on your own, even though you do have a part to play in the process. Many others have gone through comparable struggles and have read a tonne of resources on how to overcome them. By learning from others, you can quickly uncover a lot about who you are and how you can finally get over your obstacles.

Benefits of Increasing Self-Esteem

The benefits of developing a strong and healthy level of self-esteem cannot be overstated. It will be simpler for you to recognize how crucial it is to prioritize your sense of worth and all the advantages it will bring about in your life—including more drive for the future—once you are aware of these benefits. The following are some benefits of increasing your self-esteem, which you can focus on when you're a teenager.

Greater scholastic standing It is rare for a student's poor performance in extracurricular activities, sports, or academics at school to be primarily caused by their low IQ. Usually, outside factors have a big impact on how well you succeed. Growing up in a difficult environment where you are regularly teased or ignored can undermine your belief in your own ability to succeed. Regardless of your background or environment, making the effort to boost your confidence will undoubtedly enhance your performance overall.

A mentally sound state: A stronger and more robust mental state is the result of a happier mind. Positive thinking suppresses negative thoughts, which in turn prevents physical ailments and mental health problems. People stay mentally fit by participating in a range of physical activities. The best muscles to strengthen for your mental health are those related to confidence. Gaining confidence turns into a superpower that shields you from harmful energy that comes from the outside as well as the inside. Horrible things will inevitably occur at some point. Instead of merely expecting to be in a healthy mental state, the most crucial thing to learn is how to react tenaciously and constructively when bad things happen. Maintaining your confidence in the face of adversity will keep you from thinking negatively and acting destructively. Genuinely confident people don't seem to be as prone to depression or suicide ideas.

Enhanced capacity to create and maintain friends: Have you ever noticed how charismatic and confident people tend to draw friends more frequently?

People find it unpleasant being around you when you're uncomfortable with yourself, and you either intentionally or unintentionally ignore yourself. People enjoy being in safe environments. Also, because they are brave enough to voice their opinions and be open about their desires and true feelings, confident people tend to form more genuine friendships. As a teenager, you've probably observed that there's a lot of pressure to fit in. You may be tempted to pretend to be someone you're not because you feel the urge to fit in somewhere. Since no one will know who you are, this can be extremely draining and leave you feeling invisible and alone. Once you have confidence under control, it will enable you to have the guts to be authentic and comfortable in your own skin.

Improved stress management: The major cause of stress is feeling like you can't keep up with life or the amount of tasks you have to complete. It has to do with managing insufficiently to meet the demands of life and what it asks of you. Once you gain confidence, the negative, anxious thoughts fade away and are replaced with the reassuring conviction that you are good enough, that you have what it takes to succeed, and that you can definitely achieve everything you set your mind and heart to.

Elevated emotional intelligence: Emotional intelligence refers to the capacity to comprehend and express your own feelings as well as those of others. Being certain of your feelings and knowing how to express them to others can be challenging when you lack confidence. Having high emotional intelligence makes it easier for you to resolve disputes and establish stronger bonds with other people. A common cause of miscommunications is our incapacity to effectively communicate and comprehend the feelings of others. You start to trust yourself more when you are self-assured. Because you have greater confidence in yourself, you begin to express your sentiments with less fear. Others are more likely to have faith in you when you are confident in yourself.

Prosocialbehavior: Have you ever been so afraid of being judged and rejected by others that you felt the need to hide in the school toilet or somewhere else you knew no one would see you? This is a common experience, and it can be made much more annoying when others think you prefer to be alone and antisocial. It is often the case, I have found, that those who isolate themselves do so out of a lack of safety and acceptance rather than a desire to be antisocial. As your confidence grows, you start to care less about approval from others. This implies that when you accept who you are, you start to feel more at ease interacting with people. You begin to enjoy the company of others and feel comfortable exhibiting prosocialbehaviors on a daily basis.

Positivity about yourself: Self-esteem is a result of confidence. You don't hold yourself responsible for your shortcomings and challenges, even when you are completely aware of them. You accept the good and the bad in you. You don't define yourself by your flaws and failings. It's not necessary to be flawless at everything in order to have a favorable self-image. This is just false. Our world is filled with suffering, imperfections, and constraints. Even though you may know there are still a lot of problems that need to be changed, confidence enables you to see the best in yourself. Positivity about yourself also makes it easier for you to attract positive things and seize opportunities.

Less judgmental and critical of others: Individuals who lack self-confidence frequently criticize and evaluate themselves. They also really blame others, which exacerbates the situation. When you begin to embrace your imperfections and have confidence in yourself, you also start to realize that everyone struggles to varied degrees with the same thing. This makes you more sympathetic and less judgmental and helps you grow compassion for other people. It makes you more socially acceptable as you become older.

Increased inbound traffic with numerous chances. Have you ever noticed that folks who are confident seem to attract a lot of prospects? They are the ones in the room that stick out. Most individuals desire a friendship with them. People tend to have more faith in individuals to do tasks when they are necessary. Gaining confidence is one of the quickest methods to draw an abundance of possibilities into your life. Even if you are incredibly gifted, you may still fail because you lack confidence. Developing your beliefs will enable you to make the most of your abilities and talents and ensure that they don't remain dormant and buried.

Reduced anxiety: When you feel unprepared or fearful for what needs to be done, anxiety tends to increase. Gaining confidence will make you calmer and able to speak more clearly.

High potential for far greater success: Because confidence inspires people to believe in you, you will undoubtedly achieve greater success. You show that you have the ability to bounce back from setbacks and overcome obstacles, even when they go wrong. Many people never fulfill their aspirations because they lack self-confidence and, as a result, do not take the required steps toward achievement. You will unavoidably position yourself for ongoing success and an abundant life once your confidence grows!

The Relationship Between Self-Esteem And Confidence

You'll find that everyone you encounter in life who exudes confidence will have a positive view of themselves. The reflection of oneself in the mirror is your self-image or self-esteem. Your collection of self-perceptions is your self-esteem. These beliefs—and, particularly when one is young, the beliefs of those around one—are the foundation of confidence.

Even those who pride themselves on being confident in themselves can become less so following traumatic events. These experiences could be depressing things like a divorce, losing your job, being unemployed, or being socially awkward, or they could be extremely traumatic things like physical and emotional abuse, neglect, or prejudice. While certain life crises, such as child abuse and neglect, require medical attention, all emotional and physical upheavals should be treated equally. Feelings that are bottled up won't do you any good and will eventually come out. If you don't deal with them, though, they could get worse.

While depressing things happen to everyone, those who lack confidence in themselves frequently have a sensitive nature and take them much more personally. You are the only one who knows how it feels in your own skin; thus, no one can tell you how to feel. However, you should constantly pay attention to how those around you think, particularly those who inspire you and who possess the confidence you wish to emulate. You'll see that they all have the trait of never having a poor self-perception.

Given how often you've made mistakes, how many people you've let hurt you, and how much you could have done but chose not to, how can you possibly feel good about yourself? According to one ideology, you should consider your current self to be someone who has already passed away. Give yourself a fresh start instead. Restart yourself from scratch. Jot down all of your positive attributes. Consult your friends and relatives if you think your list will be short at first. Choose companions who will empathize with you rather than those who might later try to undermine you or take advantage of your shortcomings.

Take a personality test. They are always able to point out to you a fresh, admirable quality about you that you were previously unaware of. Make a note of all the good things about you and carry it with you throughout the day. You give yourself credit all day long, but your overall perspective on life is usually self-destructive and unhelpful, which obscures your optimistic and upbeat views. Jot down everything that you and your day have in common that made you feel good about yourself. It could be anything as simple as setting the toilet seat down or lending a hand to a stranger. Alternatively, it could be a personal trait or a professional quality you are proud of. From that list, you can strengthen yourself and discover new avenues for achieving your goals. Your characteristics, both good and bad, are the parts that constitute you, the puzzle pieces that complete the picture of who you are. I'm not really sure, but perhaps you could adjust the tone a bit. You will never be able to put the puzzle together if you don't know how many parts there are or what they look like.

>>Click Here to Download Your Free Book!

Recognizing the Signs

Given its many forms, recognizing codependency in oneself or others can be difficult. The following are typical indications and actions that could point to codependency:

1. Over-attending to others' needs: Codependents frequently over-attend to others' needs at the expense of their own well-being. Even when it is not in their best interests, they will often go to

tremendous lengths to help or save others.

2. poor Self-Esteem: People who struggle with codependency often have poor self-esteem and turn on their relationships for approval and a sense of value. They can believe that they are unworthy of love and acceptance.

3. Fear of Abandonment: Codependent people frequently experience a severe fear of rejection or abandonment, which makes them clingy and unable to quit toxic relationships.

4. Absence of limits: Codependents frequently struggle to establish and enforce sound personal limits. They

could find it difficult to say "no" and might let people overstep their bounds.

5. Ignorance of Personal Needs: Codependents might even go so far as to neglect themselves. They may minimize or reject their own needs. Trying to concentrate on oneself could cause them to struggle with guilt.

6. Control Tendencies: Codependents may engage in controlling behaviors to try to maintain the connection, such as trying to change or correct the other person's problems or choices.

7. Ineffective Communication Skills: People who are codependent often have trouble communicating effectively. They might avoid conflict, repress their

feelings, or act in a passive-aggressive manner.

8. Mood Swings and Anxiety: Emotional instability, including anxiety, despair, and a persistent feeling of unease, can result from codependency.

It is critical to recognize that codependency is a spectrum condition and that not everyone will exhibit every one of these symptoms. However, a crucial first step in treating codependency is identifying even a few of these patterns in one's own behavior or that of a loved one.

How to Avoid Negative Energy and Safeguard Yourself Against Dangerous Individuals

These are the things you must do in order to shield yourself from toxic people and block negative energy:

Avoid being around bad vibes.

Keep poisonous people at a distance from you. On the other hand, you must keep a minimum of twenty feet between you and an energy vampire.

Establish a failsafe strategy for handling tense circumstances.

You have to respect your sensitivity and tend to your empathetic needs. Make a strategy that will help you deal with situations that will shake you to your core.

Let's take an example where you are confused and exhausted every time your supervisor criticizes or challenges your work. This issue can be handled in a variety of ways. You can raise the caliber of your output to ward off criticism. It's also possible for you to quit and find another work. Alternatively, you might become your own boss by launching your own company.

Developing a strong stress management strategy will enable you to preserve your energy and deal with difficult and taxing circumstances with ease.

Pay attention to your intuition and your heart.

Remember that individuals are not always who they seem to be. People wear a wide variety of masks in our environment. To obtain what they desire, a lot of people pretend to be someone they are not.

You have to follow your intuition and heart if you want to safeguard your energy. Take your time forming friendships. Make an effort to gauge someone's energy before you give yourself away. If you are receiving unpleasant vibes from him or her, avoid them.

You should have enough self-respect to turn away from anything that depletes your vitality and brings you down.

Refrain from taking things personally.

Neural numbing is one of the finest defenses against harmful radiation. You need to put an end to your personal attacks. Recall that those who are harmed also harm others. The harmful and poisonous actions of others have no bearing on you.

You are sparing yourself needless pain when you stop taking things personally.

Engage in guerilla meditation.

One of the most popular buzzwords in the "new age" sector right now is meditation. It goes beyond that, though.

Concentrating on a word, vision, object, or even a person is an old practice known as meditation. It can help you focus better and enhance your mind, among other things.

Try guerilla meditation if you don't have much time for regular meditation practice.

Here's how you go about it: Step back and close your eyes if you sense that you are in the presence of an energy vampire. Concentrate your efforts on happy memories. You can focus on an objective or a pleasant recollection. Consider your blessings and express your gratitude.

By raising your vibrational frequency, you are able to block bad energies and emotions.

Apply crystal healing.

Crystals for healing are not just for warding off narcissists. It also shields you from other poisonous personalities, such as drama queens, manipulators, complainers, and pessimists. In the upcoming section of this book, we shall talk about these stones.

Establish sensible limits.

Spend less time with anxious people. You should politely decline an invitation to spend time with someone who is harmful. Make it obvious what you will and won't put up with.

Imagine.

Close your eyes and visualize yourself wearing a protective cloak before you leave your house. You may feel more safe and secure as a result of this. Never forget the power of your imagination. Your vibrational frequency could increase instantaneously.

Recite a potent mantra.

Remind yourself not to get sucked into the drama of others by repeating the phrase,

"What's mine is mine, and what's yours is yours." The mantra "I do not accept energies that are not mine" is another option.

www.ingramcontent.com/pod-product-compliance
Lightning Source LLC
Chambersburg PA
CBHW052138110526
44591CB00012B/1776